Amazing You

Astrology

Jessica Adams

a division of Hodder Headline Limited

Sharp writing for smart people

Welcome to *AMAZING YOU - ASTROLOGY*

Seeing your future in the stars is just one of the ways *Amazing You* can change your life.

Also in this series are *Numerology* and *Spells* - there are lots more to come and you can be the first to discover them!

BITE HERE!

Wanna join the gang? All the latest news, gossip and prize giveaways from BITE! **PLUS** more information on new titles in the *Amazing You* series.

Sign up NOW to join the BITE gang, and get a limited edition denim BITE bag or an exclusive preview copy of a brand new teen title, long before it's available in the shops.

To sign up text STARS to 60022

or go to **www.bookswithbite.co.uk**

FREE! Text your STAR SIGN to 60022 and receive your free Star Sign mobile logo!

Terms & Conditions Apply. For details go to www.bookswithbite.co.uk

About the series

Amazing You is our stunning new Mind Body Spirit series. It shows you how to make the most of your life and boost your chances of success and happiness. You'll discover some fantastic things about you and your friends by trying out the great tips and fun exercises. See for yourself just how amazing you can be!

Available now

Astrology
Numerology
Spells

Coming soon

Crystals
Dreams
Face and Hand Reading
Fortune Telling
Graphology
Psychic Powers

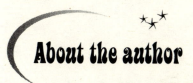

About the author

Jessica Adams is a best-selling author, professional astrologer and psychic, who has recently contributed to *Kids' Night In*, in aid of the charity War Child. She has a telepathic ginger cat called Henry and lives between her homes in Brighton, England and Bellingen, Australia.

For free Star Sign screensavers and e-cards and more *Amazing You* fun, visit **www.jessicaadams.com.** Jessica has also written *Psychic Powers* in the *Amazing You* series.

Editor: Katie Sergeant
Book design by Don Martin
Cover design: Hodder Children's Books

Published in Great Britain in 2004
by Hodder Children's Books

A catalogue record for this book is available from the British Library.

10 9 8 7 6 5 4 3 2 1

ISBN: 0340882042

Printed and bound by Bookmarque Ltd, Croydon, Surrey

The paper and board used in this paperback by Hodder Children's Books are natural recyclable products made from wood grown in sustainable forests. The manufacturing processes conform to the environmental regulations of the country of origin.

Hodder Children's Books
a division of Hodder Headline Limited
338 Euston Road, London NW1 3BH

Contents

Acknowledgements

A big thank you to Anne Clark, Belinda Bolliger, Matt Whyman, Katie Sergeant, Stephanie Cabot, Fiona Inglis - and to Nick Earls, Helen Basini and Juliet Partridge, who worked so hard on *Kids' Night In* while I was beginning to write this book!

Introduction

Astrology is an amazingly ancient (and accurate!) way of peering into the future and working out personality characteristics. With the help of this book, you will be able to make predictions for yourself and your friends, and even find out which boys suit you best. You'll discover how to choose the perfect birthday present for your best friend, and understand how knowing your family's and pets' Star Signs gives you a real insight into their psyche and their relationships with YOU.

As you read this book remember that the stars don't have all the answers. Astrology can point you in the right direction but it is only you who can make decisions about your life and your future. Use astrology alongside your common sense and you'll go far. Are you ready to find out how amazing you are? Just turn the page ...

CHAPTER ONE

You're a star!

What's your Star Sign?

Your Star Sign (sometimes called your Sun Sign) shows the zodiac constellation that the Sun was passing through in the sky on the day you were born. There are twelve zodiac constellations:

♈ **Aries the Ram**
March 20th – April 18th

♉ **Taurus the Bull**
April 19th – May 19th

♊ **Gemini the Twins**
May 20th – June 20th

Cancer the Crab
June 21st – July 21st

Leo the Lion
July 22nd – August 21st

Virgo the Virgin
August 22nd – September 21st

Libra the Scales
September 22nd –
October 22nd

Scorpio the Scorpion
October 23rd – November 20th

Sagittarius the Archer
November 21st – December 20th

Capricorn the Goat
December 21st – January 19th

Aquarius the Water Bearer
January 20th – February 18th

Pisces the Fishes
February 19th – March 19th

Which one are you?

ARE YOU A CUSP BABY?

The dates for all the signs are averaged, which means in some magazines or books you might find your sign is different, especially if you were born on the last or first day of a sign. This is also known as being born on the cusp. Visit **www.astro.com** to double check. You will need to type in your date, place and time of birth, but within seconds a free astrological chart will pop up that proves once and for all if you are an Aries, a Taurus or any of the other signs. Just look for where the Sun is!

These are the symbols astrologers often use for the 12 signs of the zodiac. But you might be more familiar with the more illustrated Star Signs which are shown over the page. Some of them look like animals - Aries and Taurus, for example, and even Leo - while others are trickier, like Scorpio and Virgo.

ARIES
TAURUS
GEMINI
CANCER
LEO
VIRGO
LIBRA
SCORPIO
SAGITTARIUS
CAPRICORN
AQUARIUS
PISCES

What your Star Sign means

Your Sun Sign, or Star Sign, reveals a lot about your personality, your likes and dislikes, and even the friends you get on with best. While it can't tell you the whole story, it's a great starting point. What does yours say about you?

Aries ♈

You like playing sports like netball or hockey, and you probably have a favourite footall team that you're mad about. Or maybe you just get all over-excited when your country wins at the Olympics. Did you know you're absolutely terrible to play *Monopoly* with? Or *Scrabble*? That's because you're ultra-competitive. You don't like losing and if someone is playing a game against you, you'll give it everything you've got. Aries girls are full of life and energy, and when you were little your mum and dad probably had trouble keeping you in your playpen. You get fidgety and restless if you're made to sit still for too long, and even long films can be boring, unless they're full of action. Aries girls make excellent policewomen, firefighters and businesswomen. You could also end up as a top athlete!

Your colour	Red
Your number	One
Your strengths	Bravery
Your weaknesses	Bad temper

Taurus ♉

Your favourite possessions really matter to you, but you can also do without money altogether and give it all away to charity. You have a gift for making extra money and finding bargains, and even swapping your stuff with your friends could prove how clever you are. Did you know the Queen is a Taurean? Now there's someone who knows a thing or two about being rich. When you are older you might find that your boyfriends are well-off, or that your best friends are clever businesswomen who know how to make a fortune. You also have definite likes and dislikes when it comes to shoes, clothes, the posters you put on your walls, bedroom ornaments and decorations, stationery, jewellery and fashion accessories. You can even be fussy about the types of flowers or plants you like! All this could make you a super collector when you are older, or even a top businesswoman ...

Your colour	Pink
Your number	Two
Your strengths	Super saver
Your weaknesses	Stingy

Gemini ♊

I bet you and your mobile phone are inseparable. The typical Gemini girl loves to talk ... and talk. You are also very good at sending funny texts and emails to people, and you might even find yourself a penfriend too. Gemini is the sign of the twins, and you are good at doing two things at once. Do you have the phone in one ear while you are busy doing your homework? Or can you prepare dinner while you change channels on the TV and listen to the radio? You need to find time to relax, shut your eyes and do nothing except daydream, as all this juggling you do can wear you out. Did you know that a brother or sister will be very important in your life? You will either love them to bits or not get on with them at all. I bet you've got a nickname for them too.

Your colour	Yellow
Your number	Three
Your strengths	Funny
Your weaknesses	Gossiping

Cancer ♋

Your mother is the most important person in your life, for better or worse. Cancerians either have a mum who is their best friend or they get into all kinds of moods and arguments with her. You are good at mothering people and animals as well. When you are older you may have a family of pets and children to take care of, or find people who are ill or feeling blue to look after. You are very sympathetic and can't bear it if someone (or something) needs help - even a pot plant that needs water will affect you! Cancerians can be ultra-patriotic supporters of their local or national sports teams too. You cheer on your home or country team and really mean it. Food also cheers you up, and when you are feeling blue, you'll eat your way back to happiness with lots of chocolate. You love coming home after you've been on holiday - it's the best bit.

Your colour	White
Your number	Four
Your strengths	Caring
Your weaknesses	Clingy

Leo ♌

You are really a bit of a show-off, and by the time you are sixteen you may have found a special hobby, interest or talent to put on display. It may be singing, dancing, acting, writing stories, being brilliant at sport, or some other kind of unusual ability, like painting, that gets you a lot of attention. Leos are happiest when they are being creative so if you want to cheer yourself up, make sure that you are expressing your personality through something you make or perform. Madonna is a Leo, so who knows, you could end up being a superstar! You are very proud and hate being embarrassed in front of other people, being bottom of the class, or coming last. Try not to lose your modesty if you do well at anything, even though it won't be easy, as you like letting other people see that you're special.

Your colour	Gold
Your number	Five
Your strengths	Creativity
Your weaknesses	Vanity

Virgo ♍

Your health and wellbeing are very important to how you feel about almost everything. When you've got a cold it can take you ages to feel normal again, so lots of Virgo girls learn good health rules in order to feel balanced. Lots of fruit and vegetables suit you (as long as you are not allergic to any of them) and so do huge glasses of water, and daily exercise. You are very good at organizing, tidying and sorting things out if you are typical of your sign, and your bedroom or schoolbag will never be messy for long. When you are older you might even become quite well-known for your beautifully clean house! You are clever at school work, not just because you have a quick mind, but also because you do the homework properly and keep your work neat and correct. You definitely don't like mistakes!

Your colour	Dark blue
Your number	Six
Your strengths	Tidy
Your weaknesses	Fussy

Libra ♎

You need a best friend, or even a boyfriend, much more than other girls do. It's unusual to see a Libran girl by herself because you like to travel in twos. You can be quite romantic and soppy about your favourite pop idols or TV and film stars, and when you are older you could fall in love more often (or more heavily) than your friends. Fashion magazines, art books, drawing, shopping for clothes and even designing clothes are all appealing to you because Librans have a strong sense of beauty. Arguments and fights really put you off because you like everyone to be friends and get on. If there is a feud within your family or in your class, you'll always try to smooth things over. You are good at patching up fights between friends. When you are older you would make an excellent political diplomat.

Your colour	Light blue
Your number	Seven
Your strengths	Diplomatic
Your weaknesses	Soppy

Scorpio ♏

You are very good at keeping secrets, and even your best friend won't know some of the things that you truly feel. Do you have typical Scorpio eyes? Look in the mirror. It's a special way of staring, or looking, at other people that makes them feel as if you are viewing their skeleton, their soul and their secrets! Scorpios are powerful people, and no matter if you have a full-time job, or bring up children at home, you will always find other people are a little bit in awe of you. If anyone at school tries to do anything mean or nasty, watch out! You find it hard to forgive and forget and you can wait a long time to take revenge. Do you get worked up about things? Don't worry, that's typical of your sign too. Especially if a boy is concerned! You are a super-passionate person.

Your colour	Maroon
Your number	Eight
Your strengths	Powerful
Your weaknesses	Vengeful

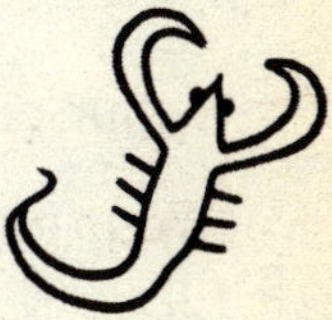

Sagittarius

You love your holidays because they give you a chance to explore new places and people, and when you are older you might even try to find a job that allows you to travel the world. You spend a lot of time on the Internet if you are typical of your sign because you can make friends from other parts of the country, or even in places which are on the other side of the world. School interests you too - not the usual boring subjects, but the projects and special lessons which give you a chance to investigate new things. You are optimistic by nature which makes you cheerful to be around. However, not everything you try will work just because you hope it will! Sometimes you'll have to just put in the effort. You can't always be super lucky, you know.

Your colour	Orange
Your number	Nine
Your strengths	Optimistic
Your weaknesses	Careless

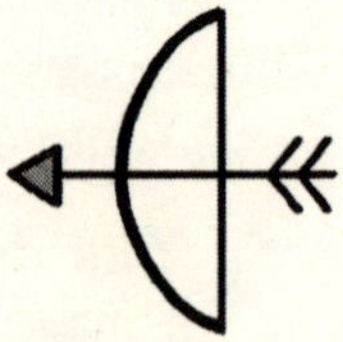

Capricorn ♑

You are prepared to work hard, and take a long time, to get exactly what you want. It might be a really good school mark. It might be a prize for a hobby or interest you have away from school. It might even be popularity! You are careful and clever when it comes to doing well in life, and although it may take you a few years, there is every chance you will find the success you want. You are less silly and flakey than other girls if you are typical of your sign, and you may even become known as the sensible one in your group. You can be a bit pessimistic sometimes. Not everything is doomed to failure you know, and not all the news is bad! When you feel gloomy you need to find some funny books or TV shows, just to get everything in perspective again. You could end up being a boss or manager one day.

Your colour	Black
Your number	Ten
Your strengths	Common sense
Your weaknesses	Pessimism

Aquarius ♒

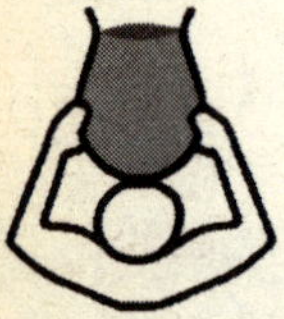

You have unusual interests and ideas if you are a typical Aquarius and you may find that you are the only person in your class, your group, or even in your school who is like this. Aquarians sometimes look different to everyone else as well. No matter what you look like, though, there is one thing about you that everyone will notice - you hate copying other people. That's why your taste in clothes, TV shows, books or pop stars is something you decide for yourself. You are very good in teams or groups of people, and by the time you are sixteen you will have a gang of friends around you who are almost like a family. You won't always join in though, or do what others ask you to do. You can be quite stubborn about it too! You have one unique talent or ability. What is it?

Your colour	Silver
Your number	Eleven
Your strengths	Independence
Your weaknesses	Rebelliousness

Pisces ♓

You are the most naturally psychic of the twelve signs of the zodiac. Some of your dreams will be quite weird, showing you glimpses of the future before they happen. You might also know what other people are thinking, or what's going to happen to them. Music, art and writing are just three areas of life where you could do very well, and lots of Pisceans are handy with a camera too. Your biggest challenge is finding the common sense to deal with all those boring, ordinary things that need to happen - like homework and packing your lunch. Having a routine and sticking to it is very important for Pisceans. If you don't do that you can run into trouble, especially when you are older. Swimming, being by the sea, or just watching a fish tank is soothing. You need the water to calm you down; try a local pool.

Your colour	Turquoise
Your number	Twelve
Your strengths	Imagination
Your weaknesses	Vagueness

CHAPTER TWO

What's your Venus Sign?

Along with your Star Sign, you also have a Venus Sign. This shows what kind of hairstyles suit you, and even what type of clothes and shoes you look best in. Venus is the planet that rules beauty and fashion, and if you look up your birthday on this list, you can find out what zodiac constellation it was passing through on the day you were born. Was it Aries the ram, or Taurus the bull? Sometimes your Venus Sign and your Star Sign will be the same, but they are usually different. So the sign you looked up in Chapter one might be Gemini, for example, but if you check your birthday on this list, you might discover your Venus Sign is something else.

As well as being the planet of beauty, Venus is also the planet of love, friendships, boyfriends and relationships. So once you know your Venus Sign, you'll have extra information on that stuff as well. So check out your Venus Sign and get ready to discover more about YOU.

Look up your Venus Sign here

1988

January 1 to January 14	Aquarius
January 15 to February 8	Pisces
February 9 to March 5	Aries
March 6 to April 2	Taurus
April 3 to May 16	Gemini
May 17 to May 26	Cancer
May 27 to August 5	Gemini
August 6 to September 6	Cancer
September 7 to October 3	Leo
October 4 to October 28	Virgo
October 29 to November 22	Libra
November 23 to December 16	Scorpio
December 16 to December 31	Sagittarius

1989

January 1 to January 9	Sagittarius
January 10 to February 2	Capricorn
February 3 to February 26	Aquarius
February 27 to March 22	Pisces
March 23 to April 15	Aries
April 16 to May 10	Taurus
May 11 to June 3	Gemini
June 4 to June 28	Cancer
June 29 to July 23	Leo
July 24 to August 17	Virgo
August 18 to September 11	Libra
September 12 to October 7	Scorpio
October 8 to November 4	Sagittarius
November 5 to December 9	Capricorn
December 10 to December 31	Aquarius

1990

January 1 to January 15	Aquarius
January 16 to March 2	Capricorn
March 3 to April 5	Aquarius
April 6 to May 3	Pisces

May 4 to May 29	Aries
May 30 to June 24	Taurus
June 25 to July 19	Gemini
July 20 to August 12	Cancer
August 13 to September 6	Leo
September 7 to September 30	Virgo
October 1 to October 24	Libra
October 25 to November 17	Scorpio
November 18 to December 11	Sagittarius
December 12 to December 31	Capricorn

1991

January 1 to January 4	Capricorn
January 5 to January 28	Aquarius
January 29 to February 21	Pisces
February 22 to March 17	Aries
March 18 to April 12	Taurus
April 13 to May 8	Gemini
May 9 to June 5	Cancer
June 6 to July 10	Leo
July 11 to August 20	Virgo
August 21 to October 5	Leo
October 6 to November 8	Virgo

November 9 to December 5	Libra
December 6 to December 30	Scorpio
December 31	Sagittarius

1992

January 1 to January 24	Sagittarius
January 25 to February 17	Capricorn
February 18 to March 12	Aquarius
March 13 to April 6	Pisces
April 7 to April 30	Aries
May 1 to May 25	Taurus
May 26 to June 18	Gemini
June 19 to July 12	Cancer
July 13 to August 6	Leo
August 7 to August 30	Virgo
August 31 to September 24	Libra
September 25 to October 18	Scorpio
October 19 to November 12	Sagittarius
November 13 to December 7	Capricorn
December 8 to December 31	Aquarius

1993

January 1 to January 2	Aquarius
January 3 to February 1	Pisces
February 2 to June 5	Aries
June 6 to July 5	Taurus
July 6 to July 31	Gemini
August 1 to August 26	Cancer
August 27 to September 20	Leo
September 21 to October 15	Virgo
October 16 to November 8	Libra
November 9 to December 1	Scorpio
December 2 to December 25	Sagittarius
December 26 to December 31	Capricorn

1994

January 1 to January 18	Capricorn
January 19 to February 11	Aquarius
February 12 to March 7	Pisces
March 8 to March 31	Aries
April 1 to April 25	Taurus
April 26 to May 20	Gemini
May 21 to June 14	Cancer

June 15 to July 10	Leo
July 11 to August 6	Virgo
August 7 to September 6	Libra
September 7 to December 31	Scorpio

1995

January 1 to January 6	Scorpio
January 7 to February 3	Sagittarius
February 4 to March 1	Capricorn
March 2 to March 27	Aquarius
March 28 to April 21	Pisces
April 22 to May 15	Aries
May 16 to June 9	Taurus
June 10 to July 4	Gemini
July 5 to July 28	Cancer
July 29 to August 22	Leo
August 23 to September 15	Virgo
September 16 to October 9	Libra
October 10 to November 2	Scorpio
November 3 to November 26	Sagittarius
November 27 to December 20	Capricorn
December 21 to December 31	Aquarius

If your year of birth is not here, go to **www.astro.com** on the Internet and look up the section on Venus Signs.

Your Venus Sign is Aries ♈

You can be quite rude to boys and you're not afraid of them at all. Unlike some girls, you like watching or playing sport, and get quite het up if someone breaks the rules! You can be a bit noisy when you get together with friends, and you'll always be the first to do something wild or outrageous. You like bright colours, stick-on tattoos and crazy shoes. You probably have a scar somewhere on your body, too. Girls with Venus in Aries are always falling over or having accidents because they are racing around, so you'll also need a lifetime's supply of sticking plasters from the chemist. When you get older you might dye your hair red, or even lots of stripey colours. You are not the meek and mild type and find it hard to be 'nice'!

Your Venus Sign is Taurus ♉

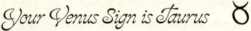

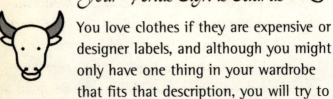

You love clothes if they are expensive or designer labels, and although you might only have one thing in your wardrobe that fits that description, you will try to wear it whenever you can. Otherwise, you can be a bit of a bargain-hunter when it comes to clothes, perfume, shoes, hair accessories or jewellery and you absolutely love sale time. You have a very strong sense of right and wrong if you have Venus in Taurus, and you know what your 'rules' are. If friends or boys don't have the same rules as you, then you can get quite upset about it. Did you know that you have a special talent for dyeing clothes, making jewellery, sewing or knitting special fashion items, or even painting T-shirts? If you didn't, maybe it's time you discovered it.

Your Venus Sign is Gemini ♊

You get bored if you have to spend too long fiddling with your hair, so your most suitable hairstyle is short, so you don't have to worry about drying it. Your hair probably goes in two directions as well, or you have two looks for it. You love lots of rings for your fingers too. You look best in trainers and the colour yellow. I bet you have a crazy phone cover too! You love doodling and scribbling and are good at writing stories or essays. But watch out for ink stains and pen blots on your clothes. You have trouble making your mind up where boys are concerned - you might like more than one person at the same time!

Your Venus Sign is Cancer ♋

Your relationship with your mum will be a big deal in your life, and you may have very strong feelings about her. Sometimes you'll feel very close and clingy, and other times you'll feel quite moody and confused about your relationship. You'll enjoy finding out about your family tree, and one day you might even investigate your ancestors and the places where they came from. Once you have found your own fashion style you will stick to it. You don't like being trendy all the time the same way that some other girls do. Once you've found your special look, you could wear it for years. The same applies to your haircut, or hairstyle. Your bedroom is probably nicely decorated, or has a clever look that you have put together.

Your Venus Sign is Leo ♌

You get a lot of inspiration from watching TV and films, and staring at posters of your favourite pop stars in magazines. Copying a hairstyle or fashion look, or even make-up, from your favourite idols is one way of experimenting with your image, and there may be something quite 'starry' about the way you look. You like glitter and sparkles, so silver or gold shoes are great, and your mum or dad probably has to stop you from wearing your best clothes and accessories out in the street. You do love showing off, and you also love getting compliments from people. You secretly practise your autograph a lot! When you wear make-up you tend to pose for hours in front of the mirror and enjoy changing your look.

Your Venus Sign is Virgo ♍

You like to look neat and clean, and wear matching colours. Dirty, sweaty trainers are your least favourite thing, and you probably stick to one or two of your favourite colours when you are choosing new clothes. You take a lot of trouble with your hair, too, if you are a typical Venus in Virgo girl, and you don't mind fiddling around with it. If you really like someone you will let them know by offering to do favours for them, or help them - often with their homework. A boy can usually tell you have a secret crush on him because you offer to write his essays for him! You love fresh, clean, neatly ironed clothes and go to a lot of trouble before you go shopping in town, or go on a school trip, so that you have the perfect look.

Your Venus Sign is Libra ♎

You love pink, and you are the most feminine and girly girl in the whole zodiac! You probably have a best friend already, but if you don't, you will end up with one sooner or later, as you like to be with just one special person who you can share your time with. You like doing things with your 'twin' friend or even boyfriend - shopping, hanging out, swapping your favourite stuff - and you become quite lonely if you are by yourself too much. Groups of friends are okay but you prefer one plus one. When you are older you might even go into business with someone, in a proper partnership. You love romantic stories and films, like *Titanic*, and believe there is a Prince Charming out there for you too! You are also good at drawing or painting.

Your Venus Sign is Scorpio ♏

You can be hard to get to know, as there are a few things about your personal, private feelings that you don't want to share with other people. Even your best friend may not know what you are really like, but that's fine by you. You are strongly affected by books, TV shows and films which have a lot of drama and emotion in them. In fact, you can find it hard to get back to normal after you've watched something dramatic on television. You have definite likes and dislikes, and know exactly what you will and won't wear, which can cause arguments sometimes. You might be one of those girls who says she LOVES or HATES things, and that's just how you feel about your clothes and hair. You like to look powerful and amazing - not just nice and girly - and you may be drawn to strong colours like bold red and black.

Your Venus Sign is Sagittarius ♐

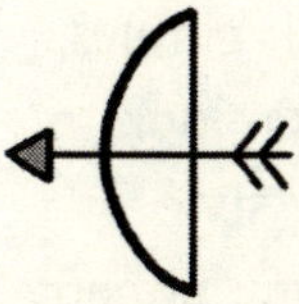

You like finding out more about people from other countries, and spending a lot of time on email and the Internet because it satisfies your curiosity about things. Did you know you have a flair for foreign languages? Try speaking French one day and see what happens! You might also like to try foreign food, as your Venus Sign says that you could be quite talented at cooking it too. When it comes to clothes, you are attracted to anything that is a little bit exotic or different. What do girls in

America, France or even Hong Kong like to wear? You might even try accessories (like chopsticks in your hair) that are quite unusual and foreign. Anything's better than the same old boring stuff everyone else at school is wearing!

Your Venus Sign is Capricorn

You don't really like it when other girls get too silly and giggly, and you are quite good at behaving yourself properly, especially if a teacher or parent is watching. You like to be grown-up in the way you act, but also in the way you choose your clothes, shoes, bags or special hairstyle. You often look to people who are a bit older than you for style ideas. You look after your school uniform properly too, and when you are older, you will have your own special look for work, probably with lots of suits and matching shoes. People at school admire and respect you because you are either very clever with your homework and tests, or just good at problem solving. They take you seriously, and funnily enough, so do teachers.

Your Venus Sign is Aquarius

You really love to be different in everything you wear, everything you do, and everything you like.

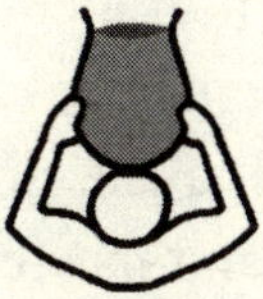

Astrology is bound to be one of your big passions in life, but you could end up being fascinated by anything from astronauts to aromatherapy! Your favourite thing is trying different perfumes and smells, especially in places like the Body Shop, where some of the money also goes to a good cause. You might get involved in charities or other groups as you grow older, and have strong opinions about the world. Typical boys don't really interest you. Your friends are probably unusual, and you may have crushes on boys who are by themselves a lot, or who have different hair, different clothes, or just a unique sense of humour. When you are older you might make your own clothes, or buy them from jumble sales or special shops.

Your Venus Sign is Pisces ♓

It doesn't take much to make you cry, as you are super-sensitive, especially when it comes to sad films, or even hurt animals. You are pretty psychic and you may have a special bond of understanding with a cat, dog or horse. You like songs and poetry and may even be good at composing lyrics. Your favourite thing is daydreaming, though, and you may have to learn how to pay attention in class. You are a bit of a softie, so boys who are quieter than the rest will like spending time with you. You like clothes for dressing up in, like floaty frocks and glittery scarves, and lots of jewellery. You'd make a good fairy! Mysterious, magical films like *The Lord of the Rings* and *Harry Potter* are your favourites and you'll never forget them.

WHEN YOUR STAR SIGN AND VENUS SIGN ARE THE SAME

Have you looked up your birthday and found out that your Star Sign and Venus Sign are exactly the same? This is unusual, but all it means is that you are SUPER TYPICAL of your sign. And guess what - you will either love people born under the same sign, or argue with them a lot.

Are you beginning to understand more about yourself from your Star Sign and your Venus Sign? Do you find yourself recognising certain personality traits? Don't worry if you don't feel that connected to your signs - they can never reveal the full story. Only YOU can know the real you: astrology can just add another dimension.

CHAPTER THREE

All about boys

If there's a boy that you secretly like (or even not so secretly) find out his birthday, and look up his Mars Sign. Mars is the planet that rules both men and boys, and it's very important if you want to know his true personality. And the kinds of girls he likes best!

When was he born?

Find out his Mars Sign here.

1988

January 1 to January 7	Scorpio
January 8 to February 21	Sagittarius

February 22 to April 5	Capricorn
April 6 to May 21	Aquarius
May 22 to July 12	Pisces
July 13 to October 22	Aries
October 23 to October 31	Pisces
November 1 to December 31	Aries

1989

January 1 to January 18	Aries
January 19 to March 10	Taurus
March 11 to April 28	Gemini
April 29 to June 15	Cancer
June 16 to August 2	Leo
August 3 to September 18	Virgo
September 19 to November 3	Libra
November 4 to December 17	Scorpio
December 18 to December 31	Sagittarius

1990

January 1 to January 29	Sagittarius
January 30 to March 10	Capricorn
March 11 to April 19	Aquarius

April 20 to May 30	Pisces
May 31 to July 11	Aries
July 12 to August 30	Taurus
August 31 to December 13	Gemini
December 14 to December 31	Taurus

1991

January 1 to January 20	Taurus
January 21 to April 2	Gemini
April 3 to May 25	Cancer
May 26 to July 14	Leo
July 15 to August 31	Virgo
September 1 to October 15	Libra
October 16 to November 28	Scorpio
November 29 to December 31	Sagittarius

1992

January 1 to January 8	Sagittarius
January 9 to February 17	Capricorn
February 18 to March 27	Aquarius
March 28 to May 4	Pisces

May 5 to June 13	Aries
June 14 to July 25	Taurus
July 26 to September 11	Gemini
September 12 to December 31	Cancer

1993

January 1 to April 26	Cancer
April 27 to June 22	Leo
June 23 to August 11	Virgo
August 12 to September 26	Libra
September 27 to November 8	Scorpio
November 9 to December 19	Sagittarius
December 20 to December 31	Capricorn

1994

January 1 to January 27	Capricorn
January 28 to March 6	Aquarius
March 7 to April 13	Pisces
April 14 to May 22	Aries
May 23 to July 2	Taurus
July 3 to August 15	Gemini

August 16 to October 3	Cancer
October 4 to December 11	Leo
December 12 to December 31	Virgo

1995

January 1 to January 21	Virgo
January 22 to May 24	Leo
May 25 to July 20	Virgo
July 21 to September 6	Libra
September 7 to October 19	Scorpio
October 20 to November 29	Sagittarius
November 30 to December 31	Capricorn

If your boy's Mars Sign isn't listed here, visit **www.astro.com** on the Internet and click the free horoscope option. Once you type in his name, place, time and date of birth, his Mars Sign will be revealed along with the other planets. Now see what information you can glean about the boy of your dreams.

Mars in Aries ♈

This boy likes having arguments with people and even getting into fights, so be careful! He is very energetic and either plays a lot of sport, or has his own favourite cricket or football team. Don't ever tell him the other side is better though or he'll get annoyed! He is very brave, and not afraid of anyone - even bullies. He might also have a few muscles, and he'll beat you at arm-wrestling every time. He has a habit of getting into trouble or having accidents because he's always rushing around and doesn't take the time to think. He likes girls who can join in with him, although it may take him a few years to decide that he's interested in girls at all. Soppy or romantic girls don't really appeal to him. He likes someone he can have adventures with!

Star match If your Star Sign or Venus Sign is Aries, Leo or Sagittarius you'll get on pretty well with the Mars in Aries boy.

Mars in Taurus ♉

Wow, he can be really stubborn, especially if you borrow something and forget to give it back! He'll nag you and hassle you until you return it, so never take something of his and hang onto it. This boy can also be very stubborn about asking for money back if you lend it to him. He's pretty good at saving money too. And he'll be interested to know how rich other people are. Being a big-earning football star or pop idol might appeal to him, or if he's the charity-minded kind of Taurean, a job on Comic Relief. He likes yummy food, nice birthday presents, and all the latest CDs, DVDs, games, trainers and clothes. If you can ever save up enough to buy him something he really wants, he'll be your number one fan. His presents for you will be pretty nice too!

Star match If you have a Taurus, Virgo or Capricorn Star Sign or Venus Sign you'll click with this boy.

Mars in Gemini ♊

He'll always be talking in class, or passing notes. He loves texting and using his mobile phone too, and he sends a lot of emails. He probably loves books and can finish something in just a few days, while the rest of the class is struggling with it. He has a brother or sister who he argues with OR is his best friend. He is a funny guy, and he'll spend a lot of his time making you giggle. However, he can also make people jumpy because he's so fidgety. He is easily bored so don't be surprised if he has lots of hobbies and interests on the go, and when you watch TV together, be prepared for a lot of channel hopping with the remote control. He likes making up strange new words and nicknames for people, so beware!

Star match If you have a Gemini, Libra or Aquarius Star Sign or Venus Sign you'll hit it off with this Mars in Gemini boy.

Mars in Cancer ♋

His family, his home, his mum, and his own sports teams are really important to this boy. A sensitive soul, he's not afraid to cry (in secret of course!). He doesn't like people or places that are too new and unfamiliar. School trips can make him feel a bit funny - the best part is usually coming home! He gets on well with girls, and he likes to have friends he can trust and depend on. He'll stick with the same group of friends because he likes knowing people he grew up with. This boy needs to have a good relationship with his family. If he doesn't, he could get quite down about it, and you will have to be a sympathetic listener. He likes his favourite food and isn't too keen to try anything new. So if you want to impress him, find his favourite apple pie or lasagne recipe and try making it yourself.

Star match If you have a Cancer, Pisces or Scorpio Star Sign or Venus Sign you'll click with this boy.

Mars in Leo ♌

When you do school plays, or music lessons, or have classes where someone has to get up and read, you can bet this boy will stick up his hand first - or the teacher will ask him before everyone else. If he is good at sport, he could be a real star and end up winning everything, or even getting his name in the paper. The Mars in Leo boy can be a bit of a show-off at times, and he might think he's pretty special! However, he'll soon learn that this makes him unpopular and quieten down. When he is older he'll try very hard to be the best at what he does, and who knows - he might even become famous! Other boys look up to him and he is normally the gang leader. He often initiates trends and other people copy or follow him. He probably likes cats a lot. He also likes the girls who everyone else fancies or wants to be friends with.

Star match If your Star Sign or Venus Sign is Aries, Leo or Sagittarius then you two could get on pretty well!

Mars in Virgo ♍

This boy likes working hard at the subjects or interests he enjoys, and you could never accuse him of being lazy. There might be just one subject at school which he's always getting top marks in, or perhaps he has a hobby or sport after school that he's very well-known for. Other people wonder how he does it, and they think he's lucky to be so clever or talented. But the truth is, the Mars in Virgo boy just tries really, really hard at what he does! When other boys are loafing around or watching TV, he'll be practising or working. He might have to take special vitamins, medicines or not eat certain foods if he is typical of his Mars Sign. When he's older he could be quite a fussy eater. He likes girls who are sensible, quiet and down-to-earth.

Star match If your Star Sign or Venus Sign is Taurus, Virgo or Capricorn then you two could have a lot of fun.

Mars in Libra ♎

If this boy secretly likes you, then it won't be too long before you find out about it. Is he good at art? A lot of Mars in Libra boys are. He's also quite keen to be friends with everyone, as he thinks fighting and holding grudges is stupid. If there is any friction between his friends, or between people in his family, he'll be the first to try to get everybody to make up and say sorry. He is popular and gets on with everybody because he's so easygoing. He doesn't say or do the silly things that get other boys into fights, so he can be soothing and peaceful to be around. He does care about the way his hair looks, and if his clothes are in fashion. When you go out together he'll always make a special effort to look really good, so don't forget to compliment him.

Star match A match made in heaven? Well maybe if your Star Sign or Venus Sign is Gemini, Libra or Aquarius.

Mars in Scorpio ♏

It can be quite hard work getting to know this boy properly, and to reach the stage where you are more than friends. He takes a long time to really trust girls, even if he secretly likes you. Other boys are often scared of him. He also knows who to be friends with, and who to avoid. When it comes to girls, he'll already know quite a few things about you, so don't be too surprised when he tells you. He likes horror films, vampire books, Buffy and anything spooky or scary, like mysterious magic. He is the biggest secret-keeper in the world, and you may not know how he really feels about you for ages. If he's typical of his Mars Sign he'll also have a deep, dark gaze - when you look into his eyes you'll get quite a funny feeling!

Star match You will have a great time with this boy if your Star Sign or Venus Sign is Cancer, Scorpio or Pisces.

Mars in Sagittarius

You can't be all serious with this boy because he gets bored and wants to run away! He likes being friends with lots of girls, too, so please don't get jealous if he pays more attention to your friends when he's supposed to be talking to you. His favourite time of year is always the holidays, and you'll notice how different he can be when he comes back from somewhere new. Going away really changes his attitude and outlook. He loves a joke too, especially in class. He is probably friends with people from other countries or backgrounds, and when he's older he might even marry someone from the other side of the world. He loves the Internet and is quite happy browsing for hours.

Star match If you have an Aries, Leo or Sagittarius Star Sign or Venus Sign then you and this boy will get on wonderfully.

Mars in Capricorn ♑

This boy secretly wants to be top in sport, popularity or lessons and the funny thing is, he will be! He tries harder than other boys which is part of his success. He also has strong ideas about what he wants to be when he grows up, where he wants to live, and even if he wants to be married, and how many children he wants to have. Of all the boys you know, he is probably one of the most grown-up, and he often chats to adults. He'll either look up to them, or he won't like them at all. He also knows all the school rules, and you won't catch him breaking them. He likes girls who get along with teachers, are popular or get good marks. He'll take ages to let you know he likes you and it may take him even longer to get around to asking you out. But if you can be patient, he's worth the wait!

Star match This sensible boy gets on best with girls whose Star Signs or Venus Signs are Taurus, Virgo or Capricorn.

Mars in Aquarius ♒

This boy is different or unusual. He might like weird and wonderful books or TV shows, and he doesn't really like joining in. He will be popular, but you'll always find him doing his own thing. He doesn't like the same things that everybody else does, so you'll have to be patient with him. Mars in Aquarius boys are good at science, and they like anything to do with outer space. They're not very slushy and romantic, though, so don't expect a big gooey kiss on Valentine's Day. If this boy really likes you, he'll be your friend first - and it might take him ages to show you his real feelings. Sometimes he acts as if he's not bothered at all, when deep down he wants you to be his girlfriend. He treats boys and girls the same, as his friends.

Star match This boy is best suited to girls whose Star Signs or Venus Signs are Aquarius, Gemini or Libra.

Mars in Pisces ♓

This boy is a lovely friend to have if you are upset, feeling down or even really angry about something. He is a good listener and has a kind heart. He loves animals too, and if your pet is sick or has been in an accident, he'll even volunteer to take it to the vet for you. He likes animal shows on the TV, and anything spooky, mysterious or strange. He can make up mad stories and tell some pretty big white lies about himself and his life. Did you know this boy is naturally psychic? He might have dreams about the future that come true. Don't take him to a sad film though, because he'll find it very, very hard not to cry in front of everyone. He can feel a bit sorry for himself sometimes, but he'll soon cheer up if you tell him a joke and make him laugh.

Star match Do you have a Cancer, Scorpio or Pisces Star Sign or Venus Sign? You two will get on like a house on fire!

CHAPTER FOUR

Predict the future

Do you want to know what's going to happen over the next few years? Astrology can help you to predict the future, but first of all you must know your Star Sign. (You should have found this out in Chapter one.) Then it's a matter of finding out how Pluto and Neptune, the slowest-moving planets, will affect your life until the magic year 2008, when they finally change places, and change your future again. Now read on to see if the predictions for the next few years are going to come true ...

Aries ♈

☆ **Psychic friends** With mysterious Neptune affecting your friends, some of your best pals could turn out to be mind-readers.

☆ **Changes in the gang** Your same old group of friends or sports team is going to go through some really big changes.

☆ **Foreign adventures** You will either travel and have foreign adventures or find someone from overseas comes into your life.

☆ **Study obsession** Believe it or not, there is one special subject you're going to study by 2008 which you'll be crazy about.

Taurus ♉

☆ **Funny subjects!** You will become really good at a school subject or hobby, which is funny, peculiar or strange. It could even be hypnotism!

☆ **Strange teachers** Most teachers are secretly strange, but you'll have one who is psychic, mysterious or disappears a lot.

☆ **Money, money, money** You will lend or borrow money and it could cause problems unless it is paid straight back.

☆ **Family favours** Someone in your family has some money or special gifts to pass onto you, maybe even in their will.

Gemini ♊

☆ **Best pals forever?** If you work very hard at a special friendship or relationship then you could know each other for decades to come.

☆ **Travel and trips** You will travel to places where there is a lot of water around you, like an exotic island, a beautiful beach, or even a resort with a spa.

☆ **Friends from far away** You will make a new friend who is very different from you, and has a different accent or even speaks another language.

☆ **University dreams** You will meet people who have been to university or even taught there and have some big daydreams about going yourself.

Cancer ♋

☆ **Mysterious money** You will gain money in mysterious or unexpected ways in the next few years. Some it could come from your family too.

☆ **Spooky and strange** Don't be surprised if you are fascinated by spooky and strange subjects in the next few years. It's due to Neptune in Aquarius.

☆ **Food changes** You will slowly start to eat different food in the future and find some healthy new recipes to try.

☆ **Exercise and fitness** You may become really keen on a different kind of sport or activity that you haven't tried yet. You could become very good at it too!

Leo ♌

☆ **Unusual people alert!** Your best friend or boyfriend in the next few years will be a very unusual person with a big imagination.

☆ **Mad on hobbies** You will go mad on your hobbies by 2008 and could turn out to be a talented artist, singer, writer, actress or sports star.

☆ **Secret crushes** Don't be too worried if you get a huge secret crush on a boy. Wait until you feel calmer about it before deciding if it's true or not!

☆ **Babysitting and child minding** Did you know that you will be given special responsibility for looking after a child much younger than you?

Virgo ♍

☆ **House and flat changes** Your parents have already moved or decorated once, but guess what? It's all going to happen again before 2008.

☆ **New family rules** Big changes in your family mean new rules for everyone, so make sure you know what they are.

☆ **Secret ancestors** Do you know much about your family tree? Some secrets about your family or ancestors are going to be discovered.

☆ **Healthy you** Virgos are naturally health-conscious but in the next few years you'll have special new decisions to make about what you eat and what lifestyle you follow.

Libra ♎

☆ **Brother/sister changes** You might think you know a brother or sister really well but big changes in their lives will surprise you.

☆ **Amazing phones** You will own one or more amazing phones by 2008 that will perform tricks beyond your imagination.

☆ **Special talents** You are about to discover a special talent, like photography or acting, that will fascinate you for years to come.

☆ **Daydreaming alert!** With Neptune in your boy zone, you are prone to daydreaming about boys that you like. Just don't nod off in class!

Scorpio ♏

☆ **Money rules** You will learn special new rules about spending, earning and saving money between now and 2008, so get ready to become a financial genius!

☆ **Family mystery** There is something mysterious, secret or unknown about someone in your family, or even your family tree, that will be discovered.

☆ **Home improvements** Your home will be decorated or renovated, or your family might even move, in the next few years.

☆ **Water, water!** Some of the home decorations or improvements will involve having a fish tank, a better bath, a pond, a pool or a new shower.

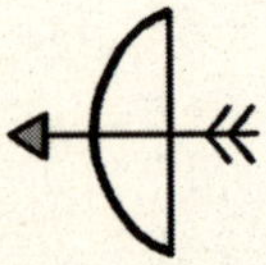

Sagittarius

☆ **Unrecognizable you** Pluto, the planet of change, is in your own sign, so it's YOU who's going to change. We won't recognize the old you by 2008.

☆ **Powerful you** Thanks to your friends, your family, or changes that happen at school, other people are going to look up to you more.

☆ **Strange languages** You will learn a strange, fascinating new language soon. It might even be an odd version of English.

☆ **Transport muddles** Because confusing Neptune is in your bus and train zone, you need to be ready for muddles, strikes, delays and mix-ups.

Capricorn ♑

☆ **Money confusion** Try to keep track of your money and what you spend it on, even if you have to write it down in a notebook.

☆ **Charitable you** Charities will love you over the next few years as you don't see the point of hanging onto money when others need it more.

☆ **Secrets, shh!** Nobody will know your deepest, darkest secrets in the years to come, as not only will you have a lot of them, you'll also be good at hiding them.

☆ **Strange dreams**
Don't be surprised if you have really weird, memorable, powerful dreams with Pluto in your night-time zone. What do they mean?

Aquarius ♒

☆ **Fascinating you** One or two people could become quite fascinated by you in the next few years. You will have a strange hypnotic effect on them.

☆ **Who's the real you?** You'll be a master of disguise as Neptune passes through your sign. You won't look the same in photos either.

☆ **Scorpio friends** New friends who are Scorpios, or just very powerful, intense and secretive people, will come into your life in a big way.

☆ **Changes in the group** Your old gang of friends, or your usual sports team, is going to be transformed by 2008, but it will all happen slowly.

Pisces ♓

☆ **Psychic you** Pisceans are naturally very psychic anyway, but over the next few years you will be astounded at your future-guessing ability.

☆ **Sensitive you** Don't be surprised if you give a lot of your time and energy to a person (or an animal) who is in trouble and needs your help.

☆ **School success** School success is going to come your way after you pour all your efforts into getting good marks, or a special school position.

☆ **Powerful teachers** You will be strongly affected by a teacher or headteacher who has amazing control over everybody. Don't try to fool this person though.

Perhaps you could note down the predictions for your Star Sign in a special notebook and hide it away somewhere until 2008. Then you can hunt it down and see just how many of them have come true.

The future is full of amazing possibilities and exciting opportunities. Using astrology to see into the future is a powerful way to glimpse the changes ahead. However, you're ultimately the one in charge here. Only you have the power to make decisions about how you live your life and your future destiny. Use your common sense and intuition as well as help from the stars and you'll be amazed at the results!

CHAPTER FIVE

Retrograde planets

Of course planets don't really go retrograde or backwards. It's just that sometimes they look as if they are, from our view of them on Earth. Whenever this happens, peculiar things also happen down here on Earth. Just look at Mercury, for example. Because it rules the things that make us tick, like cars, computers and telephones, when it is retrograde, or appearing to go backwards, we all end up in total chaos!

More on Mercury

Mercury is the planet that rules computers, vehicles, spaceships, the post office, faxes, telephones and all kinds of communication and transport. Whenever Mercury appears to be going backwards in the sky, things have a habit of going wrong. You can make your life easier by trying to avoid long distance journeys, for example, when Mercury is in retrograde. Here is a list of all the future times that Mercury Madness is going to take over.

MERCURY MADNESS DATES

2004

April 6 to April 30
August 10 to September 2
November 30 to December 20

2005

March 20 to April 12
July 23 to August 16
November 14 to December 4

2006

March 2 to March 25
July 4 to July 29
October 28 to November 18

For Mercury Madness dates beyond 2006 visit **www.jessicaadams.com** and send me an email with the header AMAZING YOU - MERCURY DATES! and I can tell you more ...

WHEN MERCURY STRIKES

- Email viruses attack your computer.
- Your computer blows up.
- The postman delivers your letters to the wrong address.
- The weather goes crazy and causes big traffic jams.
- Electricity problems make the power go out.

- Spaceships take off and blow up.
- People go away for weeks and can't be traced.
- You get more wrong phone numbers than usual.
- Letters you are expecting don't turn up.

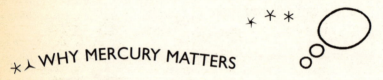

WHY MERCURY MATTERS

In astrology, Mercury (also known as Hermes) is the Messenger of the Gods. This planet is symbolised by a man with wings on his heels and wings on his helmet. Our ancestors were trying to explain that this planet was all about speed, travel and messages (and messengers.) Funnily enough, they were right. And astrologers still use this symbol for Mercury today, because it works just as well now as it did then. Whenever Mercury appears to go backwards in the heavens these days, anything to do with travel or communication causes chaos. Some astrologers fear these Mercury Madness periods so much that they won't go on holiday, or buy a new computer, or even sign contracts. Take a good look at the Mercury Madness dates I've listed (on pages 66–67). When is the next Mercury Madness phase? If you keep an eye on the news, you'll soon see strange stories about aeroplanes, computers, buses, cars or telephones.

ATTENTION GEMINI AND VIRGO GIRLS

If your Star Sign is Gemini or Virgo, then Mercury is your ruling planet. This means that you are naturally good at travelling, talking, writing, computers, and all the other things we associate with this planet. However, whenever we go through a period of Mercury Madness, you will find that you are more affected than the other ten signs of the zodiac. So watch out!

TRUE MERCURY HORROR STORIES

When Mercury was retrograde in 2003 these things happened:

- ☆ There was a power blackout across America which meant people had to sleep on the street because they couldn't get home.
- ☆ Freak snowstorms in England caused huge traffic jams. One coachload of children on a school trip had to spend the night on the motorway!
- ☆ The worst computer virus in the history of the world was launched, which meant everyone from Sydney to London couldn't pick up their email.
- ☆ So many directory enquiry numbers were launched in England that nobody knew which number to ring!

KEEP A MERCURY DIARY

If you keep a diary of all the things that go wrong during Mercury Madness dates, you can help astrologers with their research. Try keeping a list of what happens to you, your parents, your school, people in your home town and your friends. Has a bus driven into the sea? Did a computer blow up and cause havoc in your library? Astrologers like to keep track of what Mercury is doing, so if you record some fascinating examples of chaos, please email it to me at my website at **www.jessicaadams.com** and I will tell other astrologers about it.

FUNNY MERCURY STORIES!

Mercury can cause real problems when it appears to go backwards, but it can also make funny stuff happen. Here are just a few of the things astrologers have noticed in their research:

- ☆ A poor puppy who was supposed to be sent on an aeroplane from Texas to London got put on the wrong plane. He ended up in Africa and was sent to a wildlife park! Don't worry though, he got home safely again.
- ☆ A teacher asked her class to hand in their homework and discovered that someone had accidentally put in her mother's recipe book instead.
- ☆ A baby was born in Melbourne and his mother was in such a hurry to get out of the hospital that they wrote her name, not the baby's name, on the birth certificate. So there are now two people called Molly Whitaker in the Whitaker family!
- ☆ A professor who was due to give a very important speech to his university got up on the platform with his notes, only to realize that he had left them at home and brought in ten blank sheets of paper.

- ☆ A bank went haywire and accidentally let customers with NO money take out LOADS of it from the machine in the wall. Whoops!

Introducing Jupiter!

Jupiter is the lucky planet in astrology. It brings amazing opportunities and magical people to your door. So now you've found out about Mercury and all the madness it can cause, find out more about the planet that brings good fortune.

WHEN JUPITER RETURNS

Jupiter takes about 12 years to return to the same place in your horoscope. If your baby sister was born in 2000, for example, Jupiter was in Taurus. In the year 2012, Jupiter will have moved through all the other signs of the zodiac and come back to the same place - once again, in the sign of Taurus. This is known as your Jupiter Return and it is very lucky in astrology. It symbolises a year when special things will happen, and life will open up for you in all sorts of surprising ways.

WHEN IS YOUR JUPITER RETURN?

Perhaps you have already had it, or you are just approaching it now. What you need to look for is the period around your 12th birthday. The Jupiter Return might start a few months before, or it may not actually begin until you have blown out the candles on the cake, but one thing is certain: your 12th year on the planet will bring some marvellous and magical strokes of luck. And what's more, it will all happen again, in another 12 years! So around the time of your 24th birthday, you can expect more luck. Here are some true Jupiter Return stories that might just convince you.

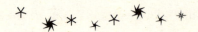

TRUE JUPITER RETURN STORIES

☆ One boy's dad got a great new job in America so the whole family moved there. It was near Disneyland, so he got to go all the time!

☆ Just four months after she turned 12, an Australian girl won a special scholarship that meant she could buy a new bike.

☆ Twin 12-year-old sisters got a modelling contract just before they turned 12 and starred in an advertisement for chewing gum.

☆ One 12-year-old boy got a new baby sister, even though his mum didn't think she was pregnant. He'd been secretly hoping for a sister for ages.

☆ During her 12th year, a girl who had asthma was given a special new treatment that suddenly allowed her to play sport and do all the things that she couldn't do before.

What will your true Jupiter Return story be? Big or small, the important thing is that YOU think it's lucky!

CHAPTER SIX

Choosing perfect birthday presents

By now you should be familiar with what the different aspects of astrology reveal about YOU. You've already found out your Venus Sign in Chapter three. Now look up your best friend's Venus Sign to find out what she really, really secretly wants for her birthday.

Your friend has Venus in Aries

Which is her favourite team? If you know their colours, perhaps you could knit her a scarf, or buy her a sticker to put on her schoolbooks. If your Venus in Aries friend likes playing sport, then it shouldn't be too hard to work out what she really wants, and that's you cheering on the sidelines.

Perhaps you could give her a set of 'cheering cheques' which mean she can count on you to turn up to support her. A lot of Aries girls like scary, exciting films, so if you are feeling really generous you could save up and get her a DVD. Make sure it's a fast-moving film with a bit of danger, though, because that's what she likes best. She'll like anything red, too.

Your friend has Venus in Taurus

A piggy bank is a good gift for this girl, or a special musical savings box that plays a tune when you put money in. You can even make her a special savings bank for her spare change, just by cutting out pictures and glueing them onto a box, and then making a slot at the top. The typical Venus in Taurus girl likes expensive presents, unfortunately, so if you really want to buy her something amazing, you'll have to save up for ages to get what she wants. Perhaps a whole group of you could put some money in together to get that special something she's had her eye on. An antique pressie would be good, especially if she knows it's going up in value.

Your friend has Venus in Gemini

She loves books, magazines and gossip - so it's going to have to be a book like this one, a subscription to her favourite magazine, or a mobile phone accessory. This girl likes running around the neighbourhood too, so if you wanted to be really funny, you could buy her a special bus pass. A set of bookplates would be a brilliant present too, as she is always lending books and forgetting to ask for them back, or even losing them. You can buy bookplates in a bookshop, or even make your own if you are feeling creative. You can also download them on the Internet, but you will need to print them out. Her ideal present? A mobile phone with a mini TV screen.

Your friend has Venus in Cancer

She'd like something old from a market or an antique shop. Maybe an old Victorian hankie, or a funny badge covered in rust. She also loves cooking and food, so perhaps you could get her a cookbook, or just a yummy tin of biscuits. This girl loves decorating her bedroom and making it look nice, so a bunch of flowers to put next to her bed would be appreciated, or even a little candle. She also likes looking after her pets, so a book on pet care, or even some special toys for cats and dogs could be just what she always wanted. Of course, if she's got a pet snake, you'll have to think of something else!

Your friend has Venus in Leo

A mirror is a brilliant present for this girl, as she is a teensy bit vain and always likes to know she's looking gorgeous. Of course, any make-up you can find that might suit her is also a very good idea for a present. She likes lipgloss and eye make-up with glitter in it, and she loves nail polish in bright colours too (though you'd better make sure you give her some nail polish remover as well, or it could stay on forever!). If she doesn't like make-up, how about hair accessories or a new hairbrush? Venus in Leo girls are mad about cats, lions and tigers, so maybe a toy cat to put on top of her desk would be just the thing.

Your friend has Venus in Virgo

She'd love some accessories to help her keep her bedroom and desk neat and tidy, so how about a tray to put all her pens and rubbers in, or a special colourful box that she can put her secret stuff in? Venus in Virgo girls love trying out things like new shampoo too, so how about little bottles of shampoo, hair treatment or conditioner? If she gets a whole lot of them to try at once she'll be in seventh heaven. Notebooks and diaries are fantastic presents for the Venus in Virgo girl, and so are pens - especially if they're fluffy, furry or have flowers on the end. That way she can't lose them, and boy does this girl hate losing her stuff!

Your friend has Venus in Libra

She loves pretty things and flowers, so you could either buy her a nice flower in a pot, or some seeds so she can grow her own. Anything covered in flowers, like a notebook or a hairband would be great too. Her favourite colours are pinks, purples and light blue shades, so whatever you buy her make sure that it's not too dark. She likes presents that are specially designed for girls, and you might like to try giving her something smelly for the bath (like a fizzing bath bomb) or even a face mask she can try at the weekend. Your Venus in Libra friend wants everyone to be happy, so whatever you give her, she'll absolutely love. She likes painting (and paintings) too, so the local art shop might give you some ideas.

Your friend has Venus in Scorpio

There is one present you could give this girl that would suit her down to the ground, and that's a big, locked diary! She keeps a lot of secrets if she's typical of her Venus Sign. It can be hard to have your lips zipped all day, so why not give her something to write it all down in? Make sure the lock and key are working properly though, as the thought of someone finding her private secrets fills her with horror. A purse to hold all her coins is also a good idea, and perhaps a red or black one would be better than pink or white, as this girl likes dark and strong colours, like flaming scarlet or bright purple. She likes mystery, magic, horror and things that go bump in the night, so don't forget to add a scary novel to your list.

Your friend has Venus in Sagittarius

What she'd really love is a ticket to the place that she's always dreamed about visiting. If you can't afford that, though, how about some foreign food, like American jelly beans, or spicy Spanish sausages? Find out where her dream destination is then see if you can find a book about it, even if you can't find the food. She's mad about books if she's true to her Venus Sign, so a book token is a good place to start. Or you could go hunting in your local charity shop for a whole lot of old books on weird and wonderful subjects. She won't mind if they're not new, as long as they stop her from being bored.

Your friend has Venus in Capricorn

What's the really cool thing that everyone wants for their birthday or Christmas present this year? That's the present that your friend wants too! She likes to feel that she's in fashion, or that she's ahead of the game, so make sure you are up to date. Chances are, your Venus in Capricorn friend already has a list for her birthday or Christmas presents anyway, so don't be too surprised if she 'accidentally' leaves it lying round. This girl is practical and she thinks it's silly not to let people know your secret birthday wishes otherwise you could end up with the wrong present! Special school and desk accessories will delight her, so stickers, scented rubbers, fab notebooks and even colourful scissors will make you popular with her.

Your friend has Venus in Aquarius

The more weird and wonderful the present, the happier your Venus in Aquarius friend will be. How can you possibly guess what she wants though? The answer is you can't, unless you're psychic. Do ask her what birthday present would make her happiest, but don't be surprised if you fall over with the shock when you find out! It could be a South American tree frog. It could be odd socks. It might be a pair of vampire teeth, or a robot. Lots of Venus in Aquarius girls like presents that are supposed to be for boys, and they certainly won't want what everybody else wants. Gadgets, gimmicks and one-off items are perfect for this girl, and guess what - she's crazy about astrology books like this one!

Your friend has Venus in Pisces

How about some goldfish in a plastic bag for your friend? Check with her parents first though. If not, fishy things make her happy anyway, so a T-shirt with fish on the front will do fine. She loves perfume, aromatherapy oil and amazing soap, so you could spend a lot of time sniffing things in the shops while you choose her ideal birthday present. She loves exotic, weird smells like tobacco flower and ylang-ylang, so be experimental. Incense is another pressie much loved by these dreamy girls. Swimming and water attract her strongly, so perhaps you could buy her a free ticket to a watersports fun park, or just a few free swims at your local pool. Fun stuff like goggles, bathing caps or blow-up boats would also make her very happy.

So there you have it - a handy guide to choosing the perfect gift. Of course you know your friend best and probably already have a good idea of what kind of things she likes and enjoys doing. But if you're stuck for ideas look to her Venus Sign for inspiration.

CHAPTER SEVEN

Family Star Signs

Do you have a Scorpio dad, or a Leo mum? What about a Gemini brother, or a Cancerian sister? And if you're a Virgo, how will you get on with your new Aries stepdad? If you're a Taurus, how will you feel when your dad marries again and you end up with a Pisces stepsister? If you're an only child, you can look up the Star Sign of your closest friend or cousin.

Here's what your family Star Signs mean. Use this knowledge wisely and don't take it as the last word. Everyone is different and while Star Signs can provide a unique insight they can never replace your common sense and good judgement. After all it's you who knows your family best! But you might just learn something new ...

MUMS AND STEPMUMS

Mrs Aries

She is one tough mum, so watch out. She doesn't like waiting for people to get ready either, so when it's time to go, make sure you're on the front doorstep.

Mrs Taurus

She is a money-mad mum, who is either brilliant at saving, or very good at having fun and spending money. I bet your place is full of lovely things.

Mrs Gemini

Yak, yak, yak! She's always on the phone or stopping in the shops to talk to her friends. She's funny though, and she'll usually laugh at your bad jokes.

Mrs Cancer

Did you know that your grandma (her mum) can affect her mood (good or bad) for days? And did you also know that she is a marvellous cook?

Mrs Leo

Your mum always likes to look her best, so she'll spend ages in the bathroom getting ready. Don't try to fight her for the mirror - she'll always win.

Mrs Virgo

She is a very healthy mum, so she might always be off to the gym, or taking her vitamins in the morning. She's a fussy eater and she likes diets.

Mrs Libra

There's one thing your mum won't like in your home, and that's arguments. She's always trying to patch things up. She loves flowers too.

Mrs Scorpio

It doesn't matter what your dad says, or even what anyone else thinks, this mum is the person who is secretly in charge of the whole family.

Mrs Sagittarius
Your mum loves her holidays and her favourite pastimes are leafing through travel brochures and practising her foreign languages on your dad.

Mrs Capricorn
I bet she's a super-successful mum with a brilliant job, or her own business. She probably runs your home as if it's a miniature factory!

Mrs Aquarius
She's not like everybody else's mum, but so what? She's ultra-friendly and is good with your friends as well. She has peculiar likes and dislikes.

Mrs Pisces
It doesn't take much to make your mum cry, and even a silly film on TV at Christmas will have her reaching for the tissues.
She loves your cat or dog to pieces.

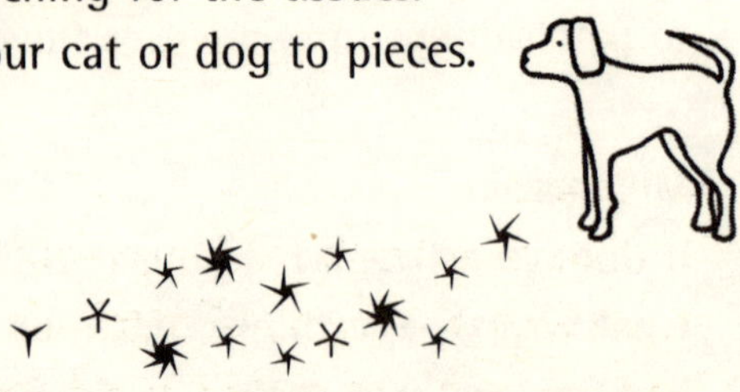

DADS AND STEPDADS

Mr Aries

This man is a dynamo, and he doesn't like traffic jams or queues at all. He either plays sport, or he goes mad supporting his favourite team in big games.

Mr Taurus

He wants you to learn about money, so every time you get pocket money or special treats, watch out, because there'll always be a lecture with it.

Mr Gemini

Your dad will always seem younger than other dads, no matter what age he is. He can do two things at once too, like watching TV and reading a book.

Mr Cancer

He'd much rather be at home with his family than at work, so he secretly likes his sick days. He likes food too, and he's quite a good cook.

Mr Leo

We bet your dad is a leader, so he might have a high-powered job, or lead some kind of group or organization. He always stands up straight and tall.

Mr Virgo

This man exercises, plays sport, or even does yoga when nobody is watching. He's funny about what he will and won't eat as well.

Mr Libra

He always buys your mum flowers, and remembers their wedding anniversary. Did you know he's a talented artist as well? Give him a pen!

Mr Scorpio

Nothing gets past the Scorpio dad. He always knows exactly what's going on. He's good in emergencies though.

Mr Sagittarius

He doesn't like sitting around at home very much, so he'll vanish as soon as the front door is open. He doesn't always want to take you with him either!

Mr Capricorn

His job is very important to him, and we bet he's been promoted a few times or done well in his studies. He can get a bit serious so try to make him laugh more often.

Mr Aquarius

He likes being with his mates, or in some other kind of group, like a sports team, a charity or a special class. He feels more like a friend than a dad.

Mr Pisces

Your dad can be forgetful and vague, and he has a funny habit of falling asleep a lot. He loves silly jokes and mad stories and he'll nick your *Harry Potter*.

BROTHERS, SISTERS AND COUSINS

Aries

They are very competitive and get upset if they lose at *Monopoly*, *Scrabble* or other games. They're tough and strong and they'll always win in a fight. Ouch!

Taurus

Don't borrow money or their favourite possessions and forget to give it back because you will never hear the end of it. I bet they're secretly rich too.

Gemini

Forget about them keeping a secret, because they love to gossip! Chances are, your brother or sister is also clever and gets good school marks.

Cancer

Cancerians are good at looking after you and worrying about you, so you'll always have someone to lean on. They get all soppy with the cat and dog too.

Leo

This brother, sister or cousin is a bit of a show-off and there will be times when you wish they'd learn a bit of modesty. They're special, though, and you know it.

Virgo

If you eat junk food you'll get a big lecture from this brother or sister, who has strong views on what you should be eating. They're always drinking litres of water.

Libra

This brother or sister is brilliant at patching up rows, or saying sorry in an argument. He or she is good at making things, or drawing cartoons, as well.

Scorpio

Watch out, because Scorpios can be rather jealous by nature. If you get into trouble though, they will stick up for you and probably save the day.

Sagittarius

They spend so much time on the Internet you probably don't see them that often! This person is pretty good at languages too.

Capricorn

Capricorns want to be popular or they want to get top marks, and although they might not talk about it much, one day you'll wake up and they'll have done it.

Aquarius

Your brother or sister is rather weird, but you will never be bored. They have a way of making a rainy day at home quite exciting with all their loony ideas.

Pisces

Watch out, because this person can read your mind. If you don't believe me, think of a colour and number and get them to guess what it is. Spooky!

WHO GETS ON BEST WITH WHOM

In your family, you may find that ...

- Aries gets on with Leo and Sagittarius.
- Taurus gets on with Virgo and Capricorn.
- Gemini gets on with Libra and Aquarius.
- Cancer gets on with Scorpio and Pisces.
- Leo gets on with Sagittarius and Aries.
- Virgo gets on with Capricorn and Taurus.
- Libra gets on with Aquarius and Gemini.
- Scorpio gets on with Pisces and Cancer.
- Sagittarius gets on with Aries and Leo.
- Capricorn gets on with Taurus and Virgo.
- Aquarius gets on with Gemini and Libra.
- Pisces gets on with Cancer and Scorpio.

CHAPTER EIGHT

Animal Star Signs

Animals can have Sun Signs (Star Signs) just as humans do. In fact, almost anything that has a date of birth, or creation, has personality. The more animals are like us, the more strongly they will reflect their sign. So a dog or cat is more likely to be strongly Aries, or Taurus, for example, than a budgie or goldfish, which aren't quite as 'human' as four-legged pets. Read on to spot your pet's Star Sign. If you don't know which actual birthday your pet has, use the day he or she arrived. This counts as their cosmic birthday!

Dog and cat astrology

Aries pets

Watch out because this pet wants to do exactly what he or she wants. In fact, they will be quite pushy until you give in. They don't like being tied up or fenced in, and no matter how many times you tell them to 'Stay' they'll probably go their own sweet way. They suit a red collar, and may have a twinge of red or orange in their fur. Quite a lot of ginger tomcats are born under the sign of Aries. Dogs born under this sign love going on the back of a motorbike, or in the car.

Taurus pets

You'll have to be ready with your own food scraps after dinner, because this is one pet that won't like ordinary dog or cat food. The cats in particular can be terrible, especially if you are eating salmon or some other yummy fish. Both dogs and cats like eating nice cheese, and if you have chocolate cake around, you'd better hide that too. Taurus dogs bury their bones so cleverly that you'll never find them again. Both the dogs and cats can be very possessive about their toys, and won't let you take their favourite rubber balls.

Gemini pets

The great thing about these dogs and cats is that they are so talkative. Both dogs and cats have their own special language and you will learn to recognize their tone of voice as they develop their own way of saying, 'Hello', or 'I'm hungry!' These animals can seem young for years, no matter what their age is in dog or cat years. They also have an excellent sense of humour, and they enjoy making you laugh by doing silly things or pulling ridiculous faces. These pets love it when you are on the computer and will lean over your shoulder to get a better look.

Cancer pets

You will need to give these cats or dogs a lot of love when they arrive in your life, because they will miss their mum, and their brothers and sisters. If they are shy or jumpy, try putting a clock in their basket (the ticking is very good for dogs). If you have a cat, a little bit of butter on his or her paws will help (licking it off tastes nice and gives them something else to think about). The true Cancerian dog or cat is a bit funny about new people coming into your home. They LOVE sleeping on your bed though.

Leo pets

Boy, is this cat or dog a show-off! Many of them become animal actors on TV ads or in films ... and the rest are often seen at pet shows, scooping up all the trophies and gold ribbons. This cat or dog is very photogenic, and you'll be amazed at the beautiful photographs that come back. The Leo cat or dog is often quite well-known, and even a little bit famous, in your street, and loves being the centre of attention. Don't ignore this animal: he or she gets quite upset about it.

Virgo pets

The Virgo cat or dog is a fussy eater and it's not a good idea to give them the same old food every time. They love fresh fish and meat, and even vegetables now and again. You will notice how the Virgo pet also knows when to eat grass for vitamins and minerals - these animals are very good at healing and curing themselves. They will love the vet's attention and many of them seem to instinctively know when to be good during an examination. This animal feels very guilty about making a mess too. So make sure they have an extra clean litter tray.

Libra pets

These cats or dogs feel happiest when they have a special friend or animal companion. Even if you have a kitten and a puppy, you will be amazed at the way they end up sleeping next to each other and playing together. Libran pets need company and if all else fails, they will curl up with the TV set rather than feel all alone. These animals are usually remarkably cute, pretty or even downright gorgeous, and often have beautiful colouring or amazing eyes. They love being sketched, photographed or painted so why not ask them to pose?

Scorpio pets

This dog or cat has the real run of the household, and the rest of the world will revolve around them. The Scorpio pet may be quiet and seldom make a fuss, but it's funny how their word is law. One look from them and everyone will be running around trying to keep them happy. This pet will soon work out who likes them best in the house, and also who they have to suck up to. There is usually something mysterious about Scorpio pets. You never know exactly where they go during the night!

Sagittarius pets

It is very hard to keep this cat or dog at home because he or she will love to go exploring. This is one animal that won't even mind flying and having a pet passport. In fact, a new life in a new place will quite excite them. This pet loves to read, too. The cats, in particular, will have a funny way of sitting on your favourite books and will try to interrupt when you're halfway through your favourite Jacqueline Wilson. Your pet might be a pure-bred or a bit-of-everything breed, but he or she will have a foreign or exotic family tree.

Capricorn pets

This cat or dog is extremely patient when it comes to food and will sit quietly for ages while you find the can-opener and clean the bowl. They are good at waiting for other things too, like treats and walks. The cats can stay as still as a stone when they are bird watching or pretending to hunt in the garden. These animals seem older than they really are, almost like wise old owls instead of cats and dogs! They are always around when you need them and are very reliable. They'll come the moment you call them.

Aquarius pets

Aquarian animals are eccentric, weird and strange. They also get very excited about things. A butterfly at the window, football on the TV or new visitors to the house will see them running round in circles or making mad meowing or barking sounds. What funny little habits does your pet have? Aquarian pets always have one strange thing they do - from lying upside-down in the kitchen, to standing on top of the roof and singing. They are very independent and love their freedom. On walks, the dogs will always try to get away from you!

Pisces pets

These animals are psychic and will always know when you are going on holiday, or coming home. They can be quite funny and restless when you are preparing to go overseas, so talk to them and let them know they'll be well looked after. This is one pet who truly understands everything you say to him or her, so don't be afraid to have a chat. These pets are very sensitive to sounds and smells too. They don't really like loud TV or music, so be kind and keep the volume down. They like soft, soothing sounds and the dogs LOVE the water.

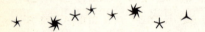

SO WHICH PET SUITS YOU BEST?

If you want to choose a pet for yourself (as opposed to the whole family) then you might want to check this list, to make sure that your chosen cat or dog shares your Element. Your Element is the special astrological group to which YOU belong. Depending on your Sun Sign (Star Sign) it will be Fire, Earth, Air or Water.

FIRE ELEMENT: ARIES, LEO, SAGITTARIUS

If your Element is fire then you are enthusiastic, energetic and full of life. You need a cat or dog who is like this too, so choose one who is born under any of the three signs in this group. Together you will love bouncing around, playing games and going for a run.

EARTH ELEMENT: TAURUS, VIRGO, CAPRICORN

If your Element is earth then you are practical, with bags of common sense. You get on best with cats and dogs who are also born under this Element so a Taurus, Virgo or Capricorn cat or dog would be ideal. This pet will be a faithful, solid companion.

AIR ELEMENT: GEMINI, LIBRA, AQUARIUS

If your Element is air, then you get bored easily and need an animal to do mad things with and have loads of human-pet conversations. Choose a Gemini, Libra or Aquarius cat or dog and you will have all the surprises you want. They'll even watch TV with you.

WATER ELEMENT: CANCER, SCORPIO, PISCES

You are super-sensitive and gentle, and a dog or cat born in your Element group will suit you beautifully. You love giving your pets lots of cuddles and you have a special psychic understanding. Your pet will just 'know' when you're coming home, for example. The bond between you two will last forever.

CHAPTER NINE

Putting it all together

By now you should know your Sun Sign (Star Sign) as well as your Venus Sign, which is like your secret second sign. If you know the birthday of a boy that you like, you'll also know his Mars Sign, which is an amazing key to his character. You should even know about those strange periods every year known as Mercury Madness Months, and even the signs of family members, as well as pets.

There are many other planets in astrology - like the Moon, Jupiter, Saturn, Uranus, Neptune and Pluto - and these can tell you more besides. If you are curious about all of this, you can try looking at your full horoscope on the amazing free astrology website called **www.astro.com.** Enter your time, place and date of birth in the space provided and in a few seconds, a wheel full of strange squiggles and symbols will appear on the computer screen: that is your full astrological chart. Don't worry if it looks complicated, you can find out what it means on the website by clicking on the different sections of the chart. There are also plenty of good astrology books out there which can help you.

Different planets, different jobs

Apart from the Sun, Mercury, Venus and Mars, which planets should you know about? Check out this list, and decode your chart.

Moon ☽

The Moon describes what (and who) makes you feel safe, cosy and completely at ease. It is all about your home, your family, and especially your mother. It gives you information about your home country, and where you grew up. The Moon can even be about food, too.

Jupiter ♃

This is the planet that shows your luck in life. Will you be lucky with money, brothers and sisters, your future home, your boyfriends, your special talents (like singing or sport), or your school marks? The cycles of Jupiter can reveal where the fun is set to begin.

Saturn ♄

This planet teaches you important life lessons. At around the age of 28, you will find these lessons come thick and fast. Are you too impatient? Too lazy? Too selfish? If so, Saturn's job is to send you experiences which will teach you better habits.

Uranus ♅

Uranus is the planet that brings shocks, surprises and strange events. The purpose of these events is to radically change YOU! This planet turns life upside-down, but it can also bring a feeling of excitement and amazement. Once Uranus has hit, life is never, ever the same.

Neptune ♆

Neptune rules dreams, psychic experiences and your sixth sense. If you are under the influence of Neptune, you might see a ghost, or have a real psychic connection with your best friend. When this planet is around, you may find your dreams can even predict the future.

Pluto

This is the power-packed planet that brings big new beginnings in your life. Conversely, it brings about a huge ending before it can give you a fresh start. Sometimes these endings are hard to deal with - like leaving your school or home town, for example. But exciting things are just around the corner ...

Psst... it's the end of the book

SO HOW MUCH DO YOU KNOW?

You should know a LOT more about yourself than you used to, for a start! And hopefully you can tell your friends and family about their personality characteristics as well. Who knows, you might even impress that boy you like with your astoundingly accurate knowledge of everything from his perfect future job, to the way he gets on with his pet cat.

As ever you should use astrology sensibly and be realistic in your aims. Your common sense and intuition will always be your best guide. Don't follow your stars slavishly and always think for yourself. Use what you've learnt in this book to improve your everyday life and you'll discover some incredible things! But before you start practising on anyone, do this super astro quiz - and then you really can call yourself an AAA (Amazing Amateur Astrologer). Good luck and have fun!

SUPER ASTRO QUIZ

How much do you know about the twelve signs of the zodiac and the planets? Here's a quick quiz that will tell you more about YOU as well as the astro facts inside this book.

1. Which is the most eccentric sign of the zodiac?
2. If you are a Libra, which sign should your cat or dog be born under, to get on with you best?
3. Which is the most secretive sign of the zodiac?
4. If your friend is good at making and saving money, which sign would you guess she is?
5. If you like boys who text you a lot, which Mars Sign boy should you look for?

6. If something weird and surprising has just happened to you, which planet is influencing you?
7. Which planet rules the clothes you wear or the jewellery you like?
8. Which Element does Pisces belong to?
9. If your cat misses his mum on his first night with you, what sign might he be?
10. Which planet is responsible for those crazy times when there are lots of traffic jams, power failures and phone problems?

ANSWERS

1. Aquarius
2. Gemini, Libra or Aquarius
3. Scorpio
4. Taurus
5. Mars in Gemini
6. Uranus
7. Venus
8. Water
9. Cancer
10. Mercury

Index